MW00676569

Inclusion

Starts With

I

Eight Steps to Inclusion: The Personal Journey

Inclusion Starts With I

For more information contact:
Renaissance Publishers, Inc.
P.O. Box 220096
Chantilly, Virginia 20153
or
The Winters Group, Inc.
2509 Browncroft Blvd.
Rochester, NY 14625
877-546-8944

ISBN No. 0-9662711-8-1
www.wintersgroup.com
www.laniersbookstore.com

*You must truly understand what
makes you do things or feel things.
Until you have been able to
face the truth about yourself
you cannot be really sympathetic
or understanding in regard to
what happens to other people.*

Eleanor Roosevelt
Civil and Human Rights Leader and
Wife of Franklin D. Roosevelt,
32nd President of the United States

Introduction

Who am I? Why do I exist? These are questions that humans have wrestled with since time began. The existential search for meaning and purpose is the core of our being.

The search, however, is meaningless unless examined relative to something or someone else. Who am I relative to nature? Who am I relative to other peoples of the world? Who am I relative to the people of my country? Who am I relative to the people in my community? Who am I relative to my co-workers?

We do not live onto ourselves but rather we are connected to all living beings in some way or another. Examining and gaining greater understanding of those interconnections leads to greater self-knowledge, the ability to co-exist harmoniously with others, and the capability to respect and value differences.

It is through the quest for self-understanding that we explore the plethora of human differences and learn to be comfortable with our selves. Self-understanding must lead to self-acceptance in order for us to accept others. Valuing self is a prerequisite to valuing others.

We still live in a world of intolerance, bigotry, and hate. Every human being on the planet carries prejudices and stereotypes about others, mostly negative. Our beliefs and values are a part of who we are. When we commit to opening ourselves to change, we are in essence committing to take a critical look at our beliefs and values. Why do I believe as I do? What experiences have led me to these beliefs? Do I understand enough to embrace this belief? What if I believed otherwise about this individual or this group?

An inclusive world is only possible if each of us is willing to examine our hearts, shed narrow perceptions, seek out opportunities to experience difference, and commit ourselves to continual learning.

The journey to inclusiveness is eight simple steps... simple but not easy.

This little book of quotes is designed as an opportunity for you to learn from the wisdom of others who have contemplated the issues of the human condition and our enduring inability to accept and appreciate difference. It should make you think, introspect and reconnect at a higher level of existence. It should help you to decide the active role you can play in moving the world towards a more caring, compassionate, and inclusive place.

Enjoy it! Share it! Grow from it! Act on it!

Mary-Frances Winters

Mary-Frances Winters

Dedicated to my mother,
Gladys Molock Smith (1917-1975)
who taught me to care,
to share and believe
in limitless possibilities.

Eight Steps to Inclusion:
The Personal Journey

Know Self First

Who am I?

What do I stand for?

What makes me "me"?

Just as everything around us is in constant flux, so are we as individuals.

We are a part of everything around us and everything is a part of us. We are inextricably entwined with the universe.

But you may go through life oblivious to the subtle changes that happen on the way to becoming who you will be. Sometimes it takes a life-altering experience for you to sit up and take notice... for you to look inward for answers to the question: Who am I?

It is a question that can never really be answered because we are constantly in a state of becoming. Just when you think you know who you are, you are no longer that person.

Becoming intimate with yourself is not easy. Cutting to the core of your essence is a lifelong pursuit. Like eating, if you don't do it, you will suffer from malnutrition. Many of us suffer from malnutrition of the soul because we neglect this part of our being. To know self, we must spend time attending to self. We must spend time alone in deep contemplation. We must be honest about who we are and who we want to become.

We cater to body and mind but pay little attention to spirit. Think about how you want to be eulogized when you transition from this world. What will be said about who you were, what you contributed while you were here?

Knowing self means delving into your soul
to find your spirit.

∞

Knowing self means that you
know that you don'tever fully know self.

∞

Knowing self means that you explore who you are
in relation to the universe. "No person is an island".

∞

Knowing self means that you open yourself
to face your dark side.

∞

Knowing self means that you are fully aware of
your special purpose in the universe.

∞

When we delve deep enough we find our best selves
to present to the world . . .

∞

The caring self . . . the giving self . . .
the compassionate self . . . the accepting self.

Knowing others is intelligence;
knowing yourself is true wisdom.

Mastering others is strength;
mastering yourself is true power.

If you realize you have enough,
you are truly rich.

Tao Te Ching
Classic Book of Chinese Philosophy
Written Between the
6th and 3rd Centuries B.C.

*People can starve
from a lack of
self-realization
as much as they can
from a lack of bread.*

Richard Wright
20th-Century African-American Author

We are a part of everything around us and everything is a part of us.

Let us be grateful
to the mirror
for revealing to us
our appearance only.

Samuel Butler, Erewhon
17th-Century English Poet and Satirist

*Before I can live with
other folks
I've got to live with myself.
The one thing that doesn't
abide by majority rule is a
person's conscience.*

Harper Lee
Contemporary American Author

We are inextricably entwined
with the universe.

Be brave enough to live creatively.
The creative is the place where no one
else has ever been. You have to leave
the city of your comfort and go into
the wilderness of your intuition.
You cannot get there by bus, only by
hard work, risking, and by not quite
knowing what you are doing.
What you will discover
will be wonderful, yourself.

Alan Alda
Contemporary American Actor, Writer, & Director

You can do abundantly more
than you think you can today if
you get in touch with your spirit,
know who you are,
step out on faith,
and never compromise.

Mary-Frances Winters
From *Only Wet Babies Like Change*

Knowing self means that you know
that you don't ever fully know self.

*The more faithfully you listen
to the voices within you,
the better you will hear
what is sounding outside.*

Dag Hammerskjold
Secretary-General of the
United Nations from 1953-61

Everything that irritates us
about others
can lead us to an
understanding of ourselves.

Carl Gustav Jung
20th-Century Swiss Psychiatrist

Knowing self means that you open
yourself to face your dark side.

*Few are those
who see with their own eyes and
feel with their own hearts.*

Albert Einstein
20th-Century German Scientist
and Mathematician

If we dig deeper to know ourselves—
into our souls—
we can release the encumbrances that
hold us hostage to mediocrity.

Mary-Frances Winters
From *Only Wet Babies Like Change*

Knowing self means that you are
fully aware of your special purpose
in the universe.

*It is as hard to see one's self
as to look backwards
without turning around.*

Thoreau
19th-Century American Writer,
Philosopher, and Naturalist

*What lies behind us
and what lies before us
are tiny matters compared to
what lies within us.*

Ralph Waldo Emerson
19th-Century American Essayist,
Poet, and Philosopher

When we delve deep enough we find our
best selves to present to the world...

*. . . the most important
earthly relationship you can
cultivate is your
relationship with yourself.*

Ken Blanchard
Contemporary Training and
Leadership Consultant

People are like stained-glass windows.
They sparkle and shine
when the sun is out,
but when the darkness sets in,
their true beauty is revealed only
if there is a light from within.

Elizabeth Kubler-Ross
Contemporary American Psychiatrist and Author

The caring self...
the giving self...

*Our energy should be spent
on self-discovery.
You would be amazed
at all of the hidden nuggets
of brilliance you would find
not only for yourself, but to share
with others in your life.*

Mary-Frances Winters

Self-knowledge comes too late
and by the time I've known myself
I am no longer what I was.

Mabel Segun
Contemporary Author
From *Reflections: Nigerian Prose and Verse*

The compassionate self...
the accepting self.

Value Self

What are my unique gifts?

Who is my best self?

Valuing self is not about boasting or self-aggrandizement.

It is about accepting that you are a unique emanation of the creator and believing that there is a special purpose that you are here to fulfill. It is about valuing your gifts. Knowing self is a prerequisite for valuing self.

We lose much of our greatness by trying to copy, compete, and/or compare ourselves to others. We complement others. I as an individual become greater when I offer my unique gifts in concert with others. It is akin to the great orchestra which makes an unmatchable sound by combining the unique sounds of string, brass and, percussion. All very different but no less valuable to the whole.

*There is no other like you. No two people have the
same fingerprints. Not even twins.
What mark will you make in the world?
How will you be remembered?
How do you distinguish yourself from others?
What value do I create?*

*You cannot value others if you do not value yourself.
The ability to respect, accept and include others is only
possible, if you are first confident in yourself.*

*Valuing self carries a certain amount of boldness
but never arrogance.*

Valuing self is about self-caring not self-centeredness.

*Valuing self is knowing your unique purpose
and fulfilling it to the best of your ability.*

*Valuing self means you have no reason for
envy, jealously or hate because no one else
can exactly replicate your gift.*

Valuing self means sharing your gift with others.

Valuing self allows you to value others.

*Public opinion is a weak tyrant
compared to our own private opinion.
What a man thinks of himself,
that is what determines,
or rather dictates his fate.*

Henry David Thoreau

*Remember always that you
not only have the right to be
an individual, you have an
obligation to be one.
You cannot make any useful
contribution unless you do this.*

Eleanor Roosevelt

*Knowing self is a prerequisite
for valuing self.*

*There has never been another you.
With no effort on your part
you were born to be something
very special and set apart.
What you are going to do in
appreciation for that gift is a
decision only you can make.*

Dan Zadra
Contemporary Inspirational Author,
Publisher, and Strategic Communications
Consultant

*You are, in essence, spirit,
housed in a physical envelope
brought to life by the breath of
God to fulfill a divine mission.*

Iyanla Vanzant
Contemporary African-American Spiritualist
and Author

*There is no other like you.
What mark will you make in the world?*

*When you are content to be
simply yourself and
don't compare or compete,
everybody will respect you.*

Lao-Tzu
Tao Te Ching Keeper of the Imperial Library,
Ancient China c.604 B.C.

*We forfeit three-fourths of ourselves
to be like other people.*

Arthur Schopenhauer
19th-Century German Philosopher

How will you be remembered? How do
you distinguish yourself from others?

When we blindly copy another's path,
we are often disappointed that
the outcome is not the same for us.
Message:
Develop and follow your own path.

Mary-Frances Winters
From *Only Wet Babies Like Change*

*I was always looking
outside myself for
strength and confidence
but it comes from within.
It is there all the time.*

Anna Freud
Daughter of Sigmund Freud—Teacher
and Founder of Child Psychoanalysis,
1895-1938

What value do I create?

*Insist on yourself;
never imitate.*

Ralph Waldo Emerson

*Learn to see, listen,
and think for yourself.*

Malcolm X
20th-Century African-American
Civil Rights Activist

You cannot value others
if you do not value yourself.

*If I didn't define myself for myself,
I would be crunched into
other people's fantasies for me
and eaten alive.*

Audré Lorde
20th-Century African-American Poet

*It seems to me that
before a man tries to
express anything to the world
he must recognize in himself
an individual, a new one,
very distinct from others.*

Robert Henri
20th-Century American Painter

The ability to respect, accept and include others is only possible, if you are first confident in yourself.

To be nobody-but-yourself—
in a world which is doing its best,
night and day,
to make you everybody else—
means to fight the hardest battle
which any human being can fight;
and never stop fighting.

E. E. Cummings
20th-Century American Poet

He who trims himself
to suit everyone
will soon whittle himself away.

Raymond Hull
20th-Century American Writer and Poet

Valuing self carries a certain amount
of boldness but never arrogance.

*As soon as you
trust yourself
you will know how to live.*

Goethe
19th-Century German Poet
1749-1832

*What another would have done
as well as you, do not do it.*

*What another would have said
as well as you, do not say it;
written as well, do not write it.*

*Be faithful to that which exists
nowhere but in yourself…
and there make yourself
indispensable.*

Andre Gide
20th-Century French Writer

*Valuing self is about self-caring
not self-centeredness.*

*It is far better to walk fully
in your own footprints
than a force fit
into someone else's.*

Dr. Johnnetta B. Cole
14th President of Bennett College,
former President of Spelman College,
African-American Author, Professor,
Consultant and Scholar

*No one can figure out
your worth but you.*

Pearl Bailey
20th-Century African-American
Singer/Actress

*Valuing self means sharing
your gift with others.*

What I am, I am.

Sitting Bull
19th-Century American Indian Chief
of the Hunkpapa Lakota Tribes

*Covet truth and authenticity.
You are who you are,
and as a creation of the
Supreme Being by definition
you are as you
were intended to be.*

Mary-Frances Winters
From *Unleashing Your True Potential
in the Workplace*

*Valuing self allows you
to value others.*

Acknowledge Your Prejudices

In what ways do I exclude?

How do I contribute to intolerance?

What are my blind spots?

We live in a judgmental world.

We live in a hierarchal world. We live in a world of haves and have nots, of better thans, worse thans, the likeables, and the dislikables.

Since the beginning of time humans have classified, categorized, segmented, segregated, separated, and otherwise made distinctions between and among groups of other humans.

Most of these distinctions are based on illogical and irrational criteria . . . where you live . . . where you were born . . . the color of your skin . . . your gender . . . your wealth status . . . your level of educational attainment, and the list of other such arbitrary criteria goes on and on.

We are all prejudiced because of the way we experience the world ... our constructs for making sense of things is based on pre-judgments ... our preconceived notions ... our understanding of ... When we don't know, we generally first think negatively.

The unknown, the different, is usually construed as negative, less than, not as good as what we already know or who we think we are.

Our values, beliefs, attitudes and world views are shaped in childhood. As humans we are capable of change but it is very hard to erase records which are indelibly etched in our minds and hearts.

Conflict, disputes, and dissention in the world is fundamentally linked to our inability to find a way to incorporate that which is different in how we make sense of the world. Our individual sense of right and wrong is inextricably linked to our tolerance for difference. We often interpret different as wrong based on our belief systems. While we have to be guided by some set of universal principles that serve to maintain order (e.g. thou shall not kill), there are too many areas of intolerance based on our prejudices, our sense of superiority and "rightness". Tribe against tribe, clan against clan, royalty against serfs, Jew against Gentile, black against white, man against woman etc., etc,. etc.

The manifestation of intolerance and prejudice may look different today than it did 1,000 years ago but the core issues are the same: a belief that there is a human hierarchy and some people are higher/better/more deserving than others.

Prejudice is personal. Prejudices are feelings and emotions sometimes so deep inside our soul that we are not conscious of them. Prejudice is not behavior but can lead to discriminatory behavior and even violence.

❧

Acknowledging prejudices is the first step to managing them.

❧

Acknowledging prejudices leads to greater self-knowledge.

❧

Acknowledging prejudices allows for a different set of assumptions and notions to be considered.

❧

Acknowledging prejudices allows us to listen to others with a new ear.

*A great many people
think they are thinking
when they are merely
rearranging their prejudices.*

William James
19th-Century American Philosopher

We are all prejudiced because of the
way we experience the world...

*Prejudices, it is well known,
are most difficult to eradicate
from the heart whose soil has
never been loosened or fertilized
by education; they grow there,
firm as weeds among rocks.*

Charlotte Bronte
19th-Century British Author

*Prejudices cannot be removed
by legislation . . . they yield only
to patient toil and education.*

Mohandas Karamchand Gandhi
20th-Century Leader of Indian Nationalism
and a Prophet of Nonviolence

When we don't know, we
generally first think negatively.

*Hatred, which can destroy
so much, never failed to destroy
the man who hated,
and this was an immutable law.*

James Baldwin
20th Century African-American Author

*What you dislike in another
take care to correct in yourself.*

Thomas Sprat
17th-Century British Author

The unknown, the different, is usually construed as negative...

*It is never too late
to give up your prejudices.*

Henry David Thoreau

Beware, as long as you live,
of judging people by appearances.

Jean de la Fontaine
17th-Century French Writer of Fables

Our values, beliefs, attitudes and
world views are shaped in childhood.

*If we were to wake up
some morning and find that
everyone was the same race,
creed, and color, we would find
some other causes for prejudice
by noon.*

Senator George Aiken
20th-Century Republican Senator, Vermont

The prejudices of ignorance are
more easily removed
than the prejudices of interest;
the first are blindly adopted,
the second willfully preferred.

George Bancroft
20th-Century American Character Actor

*Our individual sense of
right and wrong is inextricably linked
to our tolerance for difference.*

*Given a thimbleful of facts
we rush to make generalizations
as large as a tub.*

Gordon W. Allport
20th-Century U.S. Psychologist and Educator

*What we see depends mainly on
what we look for.*

Sir John Lubbock
19th-Century, English Banker,
Statesman, and Naturalist

We often interpret different as
wrong based on our belief systems.

*Our thoughts are unseen hands
shaping the people we meet.
Whatever we truly think them to be,
that's what they'll become for us.*

Richard Cowper
20th-Century British Author

Everyone is a prisoner
of his own experiences.
No one can eliminate prejudices —
just recognize them.

Edward Roscoe Murrow
20th-Century American Broadcast Journalist

Prejudice is personal.

You lose a lot of time,
hating people.

Marian Anderson
20th-Century African-American Opera Singer

*Whatever one of us blames
in another, each will find in his
own heart.*

Seneca
Roman Philosopher (3B.C.-65 A.D.)

*Acknowledging prejudices
leads to greater self-knowledge.*

*The only justification
for ever looking down on
somebody is to pick them up.*

Jesse Jackson
Contemporary African-American
Civil Rights Leader

*As long as you keep a person
down, some part of you has to be
down there to hold the person
down, so it means you cannot soar
as you otherwise might.*

Marian Anderson

Acknowledging prejudices allows us
to listen to others with a new ear.

*I imagine that one of the reasons
that people cling to their hates so
stubbornly is because they sense,
once hate is gone, that they will be
forced to deal with the pain.*

James Baldwin

*If you're going to hold someone
down you're going to have to hold
on by the other end of the chain.
You are confined by your own
repression.*

Toni Morrison
Contemporary African-American Author

Acknowledging prejudices is the
first step to managing them.

*Everybody is sitting around saying,
'Well, jeez, we need somebody to
solve this problem of bias.'
That somebody is us.
We all have to try to figure out
a better way to get along.*

Wilma Pearl Mankiller
US-American Indian Cherokee Chief

Open Yourself to Change

What are my opportunities to grow?
To be my best self?

There comes a point in our lives when we think we know all that we need to know and decide to just coast through the rest of life.

We have experienced, we have seen, we have done. We, in essence, are done... done growing!

Our values, beliefs and attitudes become fixed. We resist new ideas. It is too hard to incorporate new information that would require us to re-examine our beliefs. It is easier to just be unmovable.

Embracing inclusion requires change. It requires a constant re-examining of your values and beliefs. Values are formed early in life and don't usually change unless *there is compelling new information or life-altering experiences.*

Opening yourself to change doesn't mean that you become "wishy-washy" without firm convictions. It simply means that you remain open to the possibility that there is a better way, that new information might support the need for a new belief, and that the world is organic, not static.

There are risks with opening yourself to change. You are more vulnerable, others have a better view of your essence, you are never quite satisfied with where you are. There is a constant search for more understanding. Opening yourself to change is hard work.

❧

Change is growth and conversely growth is change.

❧

Opening yourself to change takes courage.

❧

*Opening yourself to change requires
a certain amount of self-knowledge.*

❧

*Being open to change is being open
to limitless possibilities.*

There is nothing like
returning to a place
that remains unchanged
to find the ways in which
you yourself have altered.

Nelson Mandela
Former President of the Republic of
South Africa, Nobel Peace Prize Winner

*Things do not change:
we change.*

Henry David Thoreau

We have experienced,
we have seen, we have done.

*Let him that would
move the world
first move himself.*

Socrates

*You must be the change
you seek in the world.*

Mahatma Gandhi

*Embracing inclusion
requires change.*

*Notice that the stiffest tree
is most easily cracked,
while the bamboo or willow survives
by bending with the wind.*

Bruce Lee
20th-Century American Actor and Martial Artist

*The first step in
embracing change is
embracing yourself
totally and completely.*

Mary-Frances Winters
From *Only Wet Babies Like Change*

Opening yourself to change doesn't
mean that you become "wishy-washy"
without firm convictions

*You cannot step twice
into the same river,
for other waters
are continually flowing in.*

Heraclitus
Greek Philosopher (540 B.C.-475 B.C.)

We know what we are,
but know not what we may be.

Shakespeare, 16th-Century English
Playwright and Poet

Remain open to the possibility
that there is a better way.

If in the last few years
you haven't discarded a major opinion
or acquired a new one,
check your pulse.
You may be dead.

Gelett Burgess
20th-Century American Writer,
Poet, Humorist

Only the weak blame parents,
their race, their times,
lack of good fortune,
or the quirks of fate.
Everyone has it
within his power to say,
"This I am today;
that I will be tomorrow."

Louis L'Amour
20th-Century American Author

Opening yourself to change
is hard work.

*The power to face transformation
with courage and resolve
comes from within —
from knowing and believing
in your authentic self.*

Mary-Frances Winters

*Everyone thinks of
changing the world,
but no one thinks of
changing himself.*

Leo Tolstoy
19th-Century Russian Author

Change is growth and conversely
growth is change.

*The mind has exactly
the same power as the hands;
not merely to grasp the world,
but to change it.*

Colin Wilson
Contemporary British Author

Don't fear change — embrace it.

Anthony J. D'Angelo
Contemporary American Author and Founder of
The Collegiate EmPowerment Company

*Opening yourself to change
takes courage.*

*Do not spill thy soul
running hither and yon,
grieving over the mistakes
and the vices of others;
the one person whom it is
most necessary to reform
is yourself.*

Ralph Waldo Emerson

The first problem for all of us,
men and women,
is not to learn, but to unlearn.

Gloria Steinem
Contemporary American Author and
Women's Rights Activist

Opening yourself to change requires
a certain amount of self knowledge.

I am playing with my Self,
I am playing with the world's soul,
I am the dialogue between
my Self and el espiritu del mundo.
I change myself,
I change the world.

Gloria Anzaldua
Contemporary Chicana Poet

Learn about Others

How are other individuals/groups
different from me?

How are they the same?

In our post-modern world, we find ourselves living and working with those from different clans, tribes and nations...people with whom our ancestors fought...people with whom we are still at war with today.

Beyond what we learn in history classes, many of us know little about the values and traditions of people outside of our own group. American history is taught from a very western nationalist perspective and other countries teach history with a nationalistic lens as well. Even more important than what is taught, is what is not taught. Unless we consciously seek out information about others, what we read and/or hear in the press, can be very biased.

Learning about others is a life-long journey of experiences. It is not enough to say, "I know one of them" or "One of my best friends is _____ " and think you understand another culture. This leads us to narrow, stereotypical views. Reading about, traveling to, engaging with other cultures is the best way to really truly learn about others.

When we open ourselves to learning about others, we learn more about ourselves. Learning about others shows us how we are connected as a human race and opens the possibilities for collaboration and cooperation rather than competition.

Our workplaces force us to interact with others. Our communities do not. We still live primarily in ethnically segregated enclaves.

As an individual, you can choose to expand your knowledge of others. If enough of us make such a commitment, we will move towards an inclusive world.

Learning about others is akin to
learning about yourself.

Learning about others expands our capacity
as a human race.

We have to include in order to learn.

*Our spirits are
inextricably entwined.
No matter where we
have been on our individual
journeys on this earth
or where we are going,
we are One.*

Mary-Frances Winters

The unique personality
which is the real life in me,
I cannot gain unless
I search for the real life,
the spiritual quality, in others.
I am myself spiritually dead
unless I reach out to the
fine quality dormant in others.

Felix Adler
20th-Century American Educator

Learning about others is a
life-long journey of experiences.

Namaste means:
I honor that place in you
where the whole universe resides.
And when I am in that place in me
and you are in that place in you,
there is only one of us.

Anonymous

*Sometimes our light goes out
but is blown into flame by
another human being.
Each of us owes deepest thanks to
those who have rekindled this light.*

Albert Schweitzer
20th-Century Philosopher, Physician,
and Humanitarian

*It is not enough to say,
"I treat one of them."*

We need to listen to one another.

Chaim Potok
21st-Century American Theologian, Philosopher

We must come to a greater
understanding of our connectedness.
We do not exist separate
from other life forms,
from other peoples of the world.

Mary-Frances Winters
From *Unleashing Your True Potential*
in the Workplace

Learning about others shows us how
we are connected as a human race.

*The fundamental delusion
of humanity is
to suppose that I am here
and you are there.*

Anonymous

*The sharing of joy, whether physical,
emotional, psychic, or intellectual,
forms a bridge between the sharers
which can be the basis for
understanding much of what is
not shared between them, and
lessens the threat of their difference.*

Audré Lorde

Invest in the human soul.
Who knows,
it might be a diamond in the rough.

Mary McLeod Bethune
Founder of Daytona Normal and Industrial
School for Negro Girls,
now Bethune-Cookman College

*I have spent most of my life
studying the lives of other peoples—
faraway peoples —
so that Americans might better
understand themselves.*

Margaret Mead
20th-Century American Anthropologist

Learning about others expands
our capacity as a human race.

Stereotypes abound when there is distance.
They are an invention,
a pretense that one knows
when the steps that would
make real knowing possible
cannot be taken or are not allowed.

bell hooks
Contemporary African-American
Educator and Author

If civilization is to survive,
we must cultivate the science
of human relationships —
the ability of all peoples,
of all kinds, to live together,
in the same world at peace.

Franklin D. Roosevelt
32nd President of the United States

Value
Differences

How do differences enhance who I am
and can become?

What can I learn from differences?

We can learn about others but still not value our inherent differences.

We have been conditioned to think negatively about those who are different. Civilization has evolved through empires, clans, and tribes of people who shared a common heritage... The Romans, The Greeks, the Moors, Native Indian Nations, etc. Mostly antagonistic relationships existed between and among different nations and tribes throughout civilization. The belief was (still is in many cases) to eliminate those who threatened the power and superiority of your group. In essence, we have been wired to be ethnocentric... to be anti-other... to stay with our own kind.

Such conditioning makes it difficult to naturally value differences. We have to "de-program" the message that

*different is bad or deficient. For many of us this message
is so subliminal that we would deny that we believe
it. But we expend inordinate energy conforming to
arbitrary standards of behavior, dress and lifestyle, in
essence, suppressing differences. The other political par-
ties, the other religions, the other social mores are often
considered "wrong" if they differ from our own beliefs.*

*What if we could advocate for our own ideals while
at the same time valuing others who do not share our
beliefs? Can we separate the person from his/her
position? Can we view a person of a different race/
ethnicity/sexual orientation as just different and not
inferior or deficient in some way?*

*Embracing difference creates the opportunity to
leverage, create synergy, and ultimately reach higher*

levels of functioning. Embracing difference, however, inevitably means greater tension and conflict. Opening ourselves to the tension and developing the ability to peaceably manage it, is requisite for learning to value differences.

Valuing differences means we must first value ourselves.

Valuing differences means that we listen and seek to understand.

Valuing differences means that we can hold firm to our beliefs while at the same time respect the beliefs of others.

Valuing differences requires the ability to value and manage the inevitable tension associated with it.

Acceptance of others, their looks,
their behaviors, their beliefs,
brings you an
inner peace and tranquility,
instead of anger and resentment.

Unknown

*If we are to love our neighbors
as ourselves, we must accept
people as they are and
not demand that they
conform to our own image.*

Henry Fehren
Contemporary Columnist for
U.S. Catholic Magazine

What if we could advocate for our own
ideals while at the same time valuing
others who do not share our beliefs?

*If you cannot mold yourself entirely
as you would wish,
how can you expect other people
to be entirely to your liking?*

Thomas à Kempis
14th-Century German Author

*Don't be in a hurry
to condemn because he
doesn't do what you do
or think as you think.*

Malcolm X

Can we separate the person
from his/her position?

*We have become not a melting pot
but a beautiful mosaic.
Different people, different beliefs,
different yearnings, different hopes,
different dreams.*

Jimmy Carter
39th President of the United States,
Nobel Peace Prize Winner

*If you resist reading
what you disagree with,
how will you ever acquire deeper
insights into what you believe?
The things most worth reading
are precisely those that
challenge our convictions.*

Author Unknown

*Embracing differences create the
opportunity to leverage, create synergy,
and reach higher levels of functioning.*

Every individual matters.
Every individual has a role to play.
Every individual makes a difference.

Jane Goodal
Contemporary British Ethologist

*Think for yourself and
let others enjoy the privilege
of doing so too.*

Francois Marie Voltaire
18th-Century French Author and Philosopher

Embracing difference, however, inevitably
means greater tension and conflict.

*You don't get harmony
when everybody sings
the same note.*

Doug Floyd
Contemporary American Author

We boil at different degrees.

Ralph Waldo Emerson

Opening ourselves to the tension and
developing the ability to peaceably manage it,
is requisite for learning to value differences.

*Diversity is truly about seeing
everyone's uniqueness as a beautiful
gift to be nurtured and developed,
not changed to conform to
some arbitrary standard.*

Mary-Frances Winters

Don't tolerate me as different.
Accept me as part of the
spectrum of normalcy.

Ann Northrop
Contemporary American Gay Rights Activist

*A person is a person
because he recognizes others
as persons.*

Bishop Desmond Tutu
Contemporary South African Theologian and
Nobel Peace Prize Winner

*The way you treat the person with
whom you disagree most vehemently
is the measure of your ability
to shape the future.*

Author Unknown

*Valuing differences means that we
listen and seek to understand.*

I am visible—
see this Indian face—
yet I am invisible.
I both blind them with my beak
nose and am their blind spot.
But I exist, we exist.
They'd like to think I have
melted in the pot.
But I haven't. We haven't.

Gloria Anzaldua

At bottom every man knows
well enough that he is a unique being,
only once on this earth;
and by no extraordinary chance will
such a marvelously picturesque
piece of diversity in unity as he is,
ever be put together a second time.

Friedrich Nietzsche
19th-Century German Philosopher
and Poet, 1844-1900

We have to "de-program" the message
that different is bad or deficient.

Normal
is in the eye of the beholder.

Whoopi Goldberg
Contemporary African-American Actor

Include Others

Expand your circle
to optimize diversity.

The journey to inclusion to this point has mostly been an intellectual exercise with yourself.

I have not really asked you to step out up to this point. The journey has requested a lot of introspection and learning. But at some point we have to come out, to show ourselves. What are we willing to do? What actions, what steps, what statements are we willing to make to promote and advocate for a more inclusive, accepting, caring world.

How do we include in other than superficial ways…
I made a contribution to a civil-rights cause…
I attended a worship service of another faith…
I invited some different people to a social gathering at

my home...I traveled on a goodwill mission to another country...I headed up a peace rally...I collaborated with others to end discrimination in housing...
I regularly think about the extent to which I am being inclusive when I make decisions...

Wonderful gestures. Keep up the great work.

We need to go deeper, my friends. Do we understand the interconnectedness of all life? When we include do we still view the world as us and them...as we reach out do we think of our actions as outside of ourselves or do we see that our actions are a part of a whole... a labyrinth of connections that make us a part of them...that we are all bound together...what you do to/for another...you do to/for yourself...for every other living, breathing entity on the planet.

Inclusion is about seeing the whole...how we are related...the interconnections. As we move towards our journey of inclusion, isolated, independent actions create movement, but coordinated, collaborative, holistic actions create sustained change.

How is the plight of the malnourished West African baby related to the plight of the American white manager who doesn't see himself as a part of the diversity movement? How are the concerns of Native American Indians living on reservations connected to the concerns of Aborigines in Australia? How am I connected to these issues?

Believing that all things are bound together and taking action based on that belief will hasten our journey towards a truly inclusive world.

Including others is more than superficial actions;
it requires deep understanding of our
interconnectedness.

Including others is about wholeness.

Including others is stepping out and up
to more meaningful relationships,
based on love, respect and appreciation.

Inclusion is understanding that while
we are different we are inextricably related.

*We will have to repent in
this generation not merely
for the hateful words and
actions of the bad people
but for the appalling silence
of the good people.*

Dr. Martin Luther King, Jr.

What are we willing to do?

America is not anything
if it consists of each of us.
It is something only if
it consists of all of us.

Woodrow T. Wilson
28th President of the United States

A human being is a part of the whole...
He experiences himself,
his thoughts and feelings as something
separated from the rest...
This delusion is a kind of prison...
Our task must be to free from this prison
by widening our circle of compassion
to embrace all living creatures
and the whole nature in its beauty.

Albert Einstein

How do we include in
other than superficial ways...

*If we lose love and self-respect
for each other,
this is how we finally die.*

Maya Angelou
Contemporary African-American Poet,
Educator, and Actress

*Community cannot for long
feed on itself;
it can only flourish with the
coming of others from beyond,
their unknown and
undiscovered brothers.*

Howard Thurman
20th-Century African-American Minister,
Educator, Civil Rights Leader

*Do we understand the
interconnectedness of all life?*

Mitakuye Oyasin
[We are all related.]

Lakota Belief

Humankind has not woven
the web of life.
We are but one thread within it.
Whatever we do to the web,
we do to ourselves.
All things are bound together.
All things connect.

Chief Seattle
Suquamish Tribe (1786 – 1866)

When we include do we still
view the world as us and them...

*The greatest good
you can do for another
is not just share your riches,
but reveal to them their own.*

Benjamin Disraeli
19th-Century Novelist, Debator and
England's first and only Jewish Prime Minister

Desire nothing for yourself,
which you do not desire for others.

Spinoza
17th-Century Dutch Philosopher

Do we see that our actions
are a part of a whole?

Whatever affects one directly,
affects all indirectly.
I can never be what I ought to be
until you are what you ought to be.
This is the interrelated structure
of reality.

Dr. Martin Luther King, Jr.

We have flown the air like birds
and swum the sea like fishes,
but have yet to learn the simple act
of walking the earth like brothers.

Dr. Martin Luther King, Jr.

Inclusion is
about seeing the whole...

Alone we can do so little;
together we can do so much.

Helen Keller
20th-Century American
Visually- and Hearing-Impaired Author, Lecturer

The miracle rainbow
that symbolizes our differences
also shows us that when we are
arced together in unison
we make a beautiful and
lasting impression.

Mary-Frances Winters
From *Unleashing Your True Potential in the Workplace*

Believing that all things are
bound together will hasten our journey
towards a truly inclusive world.

You lift me,
and I'll lift you,
and we'll ascend together.

Unknown

*I have seen
that in any great undertaking
it is not enough for a man
to depend simply upon himself.*

Lone Man (Isna-la-wica)
19th-Century Teton Sioux Tribe

*Including others is
about wholeness.*

*We cannot seek achievement for
ourselves and forget about progress
and prosperity for our community...
Our ambitions must be
broad enough to include the
aspirations and needs of others,
for their sakes and for our own.*

Cesar Chavez
Former Mexican-American president
of the United Farm Workers of America
(1927 – 1993)

*We are each a unique being,
but working together in teams
allows for accomplishments
not possible by any one of us.*

Mary-Frances Winters
From *Unleashing Your True Potential
in the Workplace*

Including others is stepping out and
up to more meaningful relationships.

*It just seems clear to me
that as long as we are all here,
it's pretty clear that the
struggle is to share the planet,
rather than divide it.*

Alice Walker
African-American Contemporary
Educator and Novelist

Embrace
Personal Growth

Constantly ask yourself, where am I now?

Am I growing in my journey
to be more inclusive?

What changes do I need to make?

Sometimes we think we have reached our destination in life.

We have finally arrived. There were lots of detours along the way, you are mighty tired from the journey. But here I am. I am there. Can I just rest now?

Look again. You are not really there yet. Beyond the horizon through the clouds, the path continues, the journey has not ended. Rest a moment if you must but not for too long because there is more to learn . . . there is more to do and if not you, who?

Believe that life is about learning and learning is what life is about. Continually seek opportunities to grow and develop yourself. There is always more to learn . . . always.

∽

*Embracing personal growth acknowledges
that the world is organic.*

∽

*Embracing personal growth acknowledges
that you are organic.*

∽

Embracing personal growth is being open to change.

∽

*Embracing personal growth humbly acknowledges
that we are never finished knowing . . .*

*I used to think that personal growth
was like cake. It was nice, a dessert
to the main course of life,
but not necessary.
Words like human potential
and self-fulfillment smacked to me
of pop psychology.
Now I see that growth is as vitally
nourishing to our lives as bread.*

Ellen Goodman
Contemporary American Columnist

*Beyond the horizon through
the clouds, the path continues.*

*You have to do your own growing
no matter how tall
your grandfather was.*

Abraham Lincoln
16th President of the United States

Don't ask what the world needs.
Ask what makes you come alive,
and go do it.
Because what the world needs
is people who have come alive.

Howard Thurman

The journey has not ended.

Rejoice in the constant
re-creation of yourself.
You are who you are,
but always in
a state of becoming.

Mary-Frances Winters
From *Unleashing Your True Potential in the*
Workplace

Life is change.
Growth is optional.
Choose wisely.

Karen Kaiser Clark
Contemporary Consultant,
Lecturer, Educator and Author

There is more to learn...
there is more to do...

We do not grow absolutely,
chronologically.
We grow sometimes in one dimension,
and not in another; unevenly.
We grow partially. We are relative.
We are mature in one realm,
childish in another.
The past, present, and future
mingle and pull us backward,
forward, or fix us in the present.
We are made up of
layers, cells, constellations.

Anais Nin
20th-Century American Author and Poet

*You gain strength,
courage and confidence by every
experience in which you really
stop to look fear in the face.
You are able to say to yourself,
'I have lived through this horror.
I can take the next thing that
comes along.' You must do the
thing you think you cannot do.*

Eleanor Roosevelt

*Like water flowing from
an underground spring,
human creativity is the well-spring
greening the desert of toil and effort,
and much of what stifles us
in the workplace is the immense
unconscious effort on the
part of organizations and individuals
alike to dam the flow.*

David Whyte
Contemporary Welsh Poet

*Our deepest fear is
not that we are inadequate.
Our deepest fear is that we
are powerful beyond measure.
It is light, not our darkness
that frightens us most.*

Nelson Mandela

Continually seek opportunities
to grow and develop yourself.

Say not, I have found the truth,
but rather, I have found a truth.
Say not I have found the path of the soul.
Say rather, I have met the soul walking
upon my path.
For the soul walks upon all paths.
The soul walks not upon a line,
neither does it grow like a reed.
The soul unfolds itself,
like a lotus of countless petals.

Kahlil Gibran
20th-Century Lebanese Poet,
Philosopher and Artist, from *The Prophet*

*It is not because things are difficult
that we do not dare,
it is because we do not dare
that things are difficult.*

Seneca

There is always
more to learn... always.

*Undertake something that is difficult;
it will do you good.
Unless you try to do something beyond
what you have already mastered,
you will never grow.*

Ronald E. Osborn
20th-Century Minister, Scholar, and Christian
Theological Seminary Church Historian

*The important thing is
not to stop questioning.*

Albert Einstein

*Embracing personal growth
acknowledges that you are organic.*

*The wisest mind has
something yet to learn.*

George Santayana
20th Century Spanish-American Philosopher

We shall not cease from exploration,
and the end of all our exploring
will be to arrive where we started
and know the place
for the first time.

T.S. Eliot
20th-Century British Poet and
Nobel Prize Winner

Embracing personal growth
is being open to change.

*And the day came when
the risk to remain tight in a bud
was more painful than
the risk it took to blossom.*

Anais Nin

*When you are through changing,
you are through.*

Bruce Barton
Former Chairman of Batten, Barton,
Durstine, and Osborn (BBDO), one of the
world's largest advertising agencies

*Embracing personal growth
humbly acknowledges that we are
never finished knowing.*

Good, better, best.
Never let it rest.
Until your good gets better
and your better gets best.

Author Unknown

Acknowledgements

I would like to thank the wonderful people
in my life who help me to produce works such
as this. I appreciate your steadfastness, your
ingenuity and all of those added "little things"
you do that make such a big difference.

Susan Chapman
The Winters Group, Administrative Assistant

Pam Cox
The Winters Group, Office Manager

Lisa Dumas,
The Winters Group, Executive Protege

Debby Russo
The Winters Group, Executive Assistant

Leon T. Lanier, Sr., The Winters Group, COO
and President of Renaissance Books, Inc.

Cathy Kamp, Creative Ink

Debra Atkins-Manos, A-M Creative

Mary-Frances Winters chose to ignore the advice of the Niagara Falls, New York, high school counselor who told her that attending a four-year college was "too lofty" a goal for her as an African American. She entered the University of Rochester in 1969, majoring in English and psychology. Later, she received an M.B.A. and became the University's first African-American female trustee. In 1997, she received an Honorary Doctorate from Roberts Wesleyan College, and in 1998, she was awarded the University of Rochester's prestigious Hutchinson Medal, the highest alumni honor. She has also been a Distinguished Minett Professor at the Rochester Institute of Technology.

Before starting The Winters Group in 1984, Dr. Winters spent 11 years in the corporate arena. She built The Winters Group with clients including not-for-profit agencies,

*health care organizations and corporations such as
Eastman Kodak Company, Xerox Corporation, Mobil
Chemical, AT&T, United Way, Landmark Communications,
and the Council on Foundations. In 1988, she was
recognized as the Minority Business Person of the Year
in Rochester, followed by the Athena Award from the
Women's Council of the Greater Rochester Chamber of
Commerce, and the national Women of Enterprise Award
from Avon Products, Inc. and the U.S. Small Business
Administration. In 1994, Rochester's Urban League
presented Dr. Winters with the Outstanding Community
Leader Award, and in 1996, her leadership was recognized
when she was chosen to carry the Olympic Torch through
her hometown. In 1997, the U.S. Small Business
Administration named her the Rochester Small Business
Person of the Year.*

Dr. Winters contributes regularly to Gannett Newspapers' USA Today *and* Democrat and Chronicle *and a number of professional journals.*

She has published a book titled Only Wet Babies Like Change, Workplace Wisdom for Baby Boomers, *and a journal,* Unleashing Your True Potential in the Workplace: A Journal for Self-Discovery and Unprecedented Performance. *Dr. Winters is often a featured speaker on issues affecting the workplace and diversity. She is a member of the National Speakers' Association.*

Contact Information

To contact Mary-Frances Winters, e-mail
mfwinters@wintersgroup.com
or write to her at:
The Winters Group • 2509 Browncroft Blvd.,
Suite 103 • Rochester, New York 14625

To order more copies of *Inclusion Starts with I*
go to www.Laniersbookstore.com
www.wintersgroup.com or call 877-546-8944

Contact Information:
National/International
Consulting Services
Speaking Engagements
Leadership Workshops
Video Tapes
Book Orders

Leon T. Lanier c/o
The Winters Group, Inc.
Renaissance Books, Inc.
1-877-546-8944